**Anonymous**

I am a White woman,
largely ignored,
but a very old soul.
Rarely Caucasian,
my skin is the shade of ebony, copper
or the heart of a lotus bloom.

My soulmate journeys with me each life.
Always the same colour as me.
And our babies blossom from my womb
in a beautiful hue.

I will marry him soon.
I want to bear him a child
whose skin is the shade
of love: starflower, baby's breath,
or a colour so rare it is not yet named
in the Far East or in the West.

**Glazed Tangerine**

The fruit in the bowl
is a tableau,
still life.
An apple in its skin,
a soft peach,
a glazed tangerine —
its pale sweet juice.

They bear the memory of sun
in their flesh, as I do.
My breasts are great
with the weight
of Vitamin D.

I peel the tangerine.
I taste light on my tongue.
For a moment, I know Morocco:
Mongers by the sea.
And the Far East
where these oranges
were conceived
from energy – like me.

*July 7/22*

*For Eve,*

# COLOUR
# Theory

Poems By
April Bulmer

*With love,*
*April*

Copyright © 2022 by April Bulmer

All rights reserved

No part of this book may be reproduced, stored in a retrieval system, or transmitted by any means, electronic, mechanical, photocopying, recording, or otherwise, without written permission from the author or publisher. There is one exception. Brief passages may be quoted in articles or reviews.

ISBN 978-1-55483-501-0

I wish to thank the Waterloo Region Writers Alliance for their feedback and kind support.

The photos were purchased from Depositphotos Inc. The cover is called A Stone As a Heart Lies Under a Waterfall, the other two shots are called The Word Energy and Autumn Walnut Leaves With Handwritten Text.

## Soothing Green Tea

The Sun is in Aries, the Moon in Scorpio:
I am emotional.
I breathe into my belly
where the feelings grow like a disease.

I sip soothing green tea.
I bear the mug in my hands.
It is spring, but it is snowing and cold.

The earth opens in April.
I open, too. There is a hole
in my gut the shade of the tea.

I will telephone soon:
an Easter greeting,
though I do not believe
Jesus rose from the tomb.
I want to lift your spirits,
but even the messiah
lies broken and will not ascend.

I drink the soothing green tea
as you and I speak.
The steam rises
to high heaven.

**Nourish the Soul**

I write poems
that bloom from dirt and rain.
You find them beautiful:
small plants that live in the cold and sprout
when the Sun warms the mud.

I wear winter boots until early May
when the thaw melts.
Today, my heart shivers.
It is a frozen bed.
Nothing grows from the hard ground.

I wonder if there was a period
when the Earth turned in the dark —
before the Sun crowned
from the black womb of the sky.
A long era before the birth of poetry
when the planet was silent
and crazy on its axis.
When it shuddered as I do
in the mania of its blue mind.

**Indian Spice**

Before you read the planets,
moons and stars
you were naked and white.
Your mind was a storm.
It sang songs from our country:
*"Mon pays, ce n'est pas un pay, c'est l'hiver."*
*"Je sais bien quelque chose."*

You chanted in a dark room
in India
until your words melted in the heat.

You ate curried meat and rice,
sipped chi tea.
Sang "cumin, cilantro, black cardamom…"
Your mind rose like chana masala
or lamb vindaloo.

You studied then: the language of the sky.
The houses, the signs.

You spoke of Venus and the Sun
with a poet's tongue:
*Indian spice and Hari Om.*

**Sanctuary**

There is a place in me,
a kind of sanctuary,
where the Lord lives and reigns.
I have never been there.
Today, I imagine it is chilly
for it is early spring.
He wears a jacket and rubber boots.
His feet sink into the April mud
as it rains.

The sanctuary is dim.
The Lord bears a white cane
to navigate his days.
It pocks the damp earth.
There are holes in me.
I am scarred by the Lord
like a First Nations girl
who suffered a plague.

## Caribou

In another life
I killed a reindeer
and offered its antlers
to a pagan god.

I was a woman
in the far north.
I fed you
the slender meal.
But in the shadow
of the fire
we hungered,
though we prayed
a herd of caribou
might graze.

The god was cruel.
He mocked us
as I boiled lichen tea
in the morning.
The antlers I offered him:
broken.

And I think now
of Jesus in the tomb.
For I reject the resurrection
and imagine him, too,
a pile of bones.
His disciples hungry
and hunting his ghost.

## Armadillo

I am wild, do not chain me.
For in the dream
an armadillo is enraged.
He wears a collar
and a leash.
He puffs like a small factory.

Armadillo is my totem.
I wear spiritual armour,
bony plates. They shield me
when I am weak.

**Angel Feather**

I thought at first
it was the down of a mourning dove
or a late snowflake.
I see now it is an angel feather
turning in the damp of spring rain.

My angel visits regularly.
His wings are wide and soft.
When I am weak,
he wraps them around my fat body
and hugs.

The feather has fallen now
and lies upon the mud:
curved like a comma.
I write a brief message
on the earth,
drag a twig across her skin:
*Angel, your feather*
*is a breath, a pause.*
*It punctuates my poem.*

**Pencil Sketch**

I imagine
your valves and vessels,
then sketch them
with my pencil.
I trace the lines
of your heart.
The four chambers,
its muscular walls.
I offer you your atrium,
your auricles.

## Toadstool

I imagine you my husband.
A warlock who soothes my nerves.
I gather medicines for your pot:
toadstool, tansy, the carcass of a frog.
You stir the cauldron with a witch spoon
we ordered from Amazon.

**Chinese Jade**

I bought you a wedding gift:
two Chinese foo dogs sculpted from jade.
The dogs, also known as *shishi*,
are mythical lion-like creatures.
They are common across a breath of art forms,
ranging from architecture to tattoos.

I ordered yours from Amazon.
They arrived in a crate from Hong Kong.
They symbolize prosperity and success.
To us, they represent our past incarnations:
lives lived in Asia.
The sculptures are green and smooth.

I imagine our wedding day
when I offer the dogs to you.
You are the man I married
in the Han Dynasty
when foo dogs were first carved from jade.
They were placed at the entrances
of palaces and temples
to guard and intimidate.

They flank sacred portals in the Forbidden City.
I hope they protect our door:
ward off demons and the spirit of my father.
I pray he flies from our home
terrified by the spell:
yin-yang cast from green tongues.

**Chance of Rain**

The sky is white today.
Clouds heavy as though great-with-child.
I, myself, have slimmed down.

The sun is in Aries now.
I will wed in Libra, *La Balance*,
when leaves give up the ghost.
I will offer my spirit to a holy man
whose words are medicine.
They salve my wounded heart.

Today, I pray for rain
to wash my house
and the sins of my father,
to baptize him.
May he repent
for the winters of my discontent.

**Flower Girl**

I wed my love
in a beautiful cave
lined in moss green.
Above the hearth:
a bison, its head
dipped in gold.

Libra: *La Balance*.
My dog, her collar
of chrysanthemums.

**Deep Breath**

Husband, you and I can hardly breathe.
My mother never held me.
Your mother voodooed you.

I imagine I bear you a child: a girl.
I watch her breathe.
She stirs oxygen
in the deep pot that is her gut.

You and I are not well.
But our daughter breathes
as I breastfeed.

You work in a hospital.
You are a surgeon.
Today, you watched
a woman in a mask
draw air into her lungs.
Her chest rose and fell
beneath a green sheet.
I imagine she slept so deeply
she did not dream
of drugs or disease.

Perhaps she is a woman like me
who still gasps for breath,
who exhales her mother
like a pant.
A patient who inhales
inside a surgical mask
unconscious of the rhythm
of the machine.

## Soaking Up the Rays

Today is my birthday.
I was born in the spring
when the earth still bears
the weight of winter.

My heart is heavy too.

It rained this morning
and I felt the damp.
Now the sun warms.

I am low and high.
I am the seasons.

You hold me
in the chill when I shiver.
You thaw my old soul.
It is made of weather.

## Biography

April Bulmer is an award-winning Canadian poet. She holds Master's degrees in creative writing, women and religion and theological studies from major universities. Much of her writing deals with women and spirituality and the divine feminine. Many of her dozen books have been shortlisted for awards, including the International Beverly Prize for Literature in London, England, the Pat Lowther Memorial Award for the best book of poetry by a Canadian woman and the Next Generation Indie Book Awards in the U.S. She won the YWCA Women of Distinction Award in the art and culture category in Cambridge, Ontario where she lives. April's work has also been celebrated and published widely in prestigious journals, anthologies and newspapers. For critical response to April's writing and more biographical information about her, please see www.aprilbulmer.wordpress.com Contact numbers for April Bulmer are also found there. Many of April's books are available for purchase by emailing her.

CPSIA information can be obtained
at www.ICGtesting.com
Printed in the USA
BVHW020546120622
639569BV00001B/4